IRAQ
the land

April Fast

A Bobbie Kalman Book

The Lands, Peoples, and Cultures Series

Crabtree Publishing Company

www.crabtreebooks.com

The Lands, Peoples, and Cultures Series

Created by Bobbie Kalman

Author: April Fast

Third edition: Q2AMedia

Editor: Adrianna Morganelli

Content and Photo editor: Kokila Manchanda

Editorial director: Kathy Middleton

Production coordinator: Margaret Salter

Prepress technician: Margaret Salter

Project manager: Kumar Kanul

First and second editions
  Coordinating editor: Ellen Rodger
  Project editor: Rachel Eagen
  Production coordinator: Rosie Gowsell
  Project development: First Folio Resource Group, Inc.
  Photo research: Maria DeCambra
  Proofreading: Lynne Elliott
  Consultants: Thabit Abdullah, Department of History,
    York University; Majid Aziza

Cover: A wooden water wheel among the palm trees on the Eurphrates River.

Title page: The golden dome of the beautiful Shrine of Askari, in Samarra, is covered with 72,000 gold plates and is one of the largest domes in the Muslim world.

Icon: Date palms, Iraq's chief exported crop, appear at the head of each section. Unripe dates are green in color, becoming yellow then reddish-brown when fully ripe.

Photographs
AP Photo/David Guttenfelder: p. 15 (right); INA/ CP: p. 7 (top); Itsuo Inouye: p. 27 (right); Julie Jacobson: p. 26 (top); Manish Swarup: p. 27 (left);
Archives Charmet/Bridgeman Art Library: p. 20 (right);
Art Directors/Ask Images: p. 7 (bottom), p. 29; Jane Sweeney: p. 12, p. 19 (top), p. 24, p. 25 (bottom)
Art Resource, NY: Scala: title page;
Associated Media Group: Peter Langer: p. 19 (bottom), p. 20 (left)
Atlas Geographic: Fatih Pinar: p. 4, p. 28 (top);
Corbis: William Dow/ Magma: p. 31 (top); Antoine Gyori/Magma: p. 16; Hulton-Deutsch Collection/Magma: p. 6; Wolfgang Kaehler/Magma: p. 21 (bottom); Ed Kashi/Magma: p. 15 (left); Steve Kaufman/Magma: p. 31 (bottom); Charles & Josette Lenars/Magma: p. 3; Nik Wheeler/Magma: p. 10, p. 11, p. 21 (top); Michael S. Yamashita/Magma: p. 18
Dreamstime: Cathykeifer: p. 30
Getty Images: Hazhar Arif/ AFP: p. 14 (top); Nicolas Asfouri/ AFP: p. 13; Mauricio Lima/AFP: p. 14 (bottom); Scott Peterson: p. 17 (top); Karim Sahib/AFP: p. 5 (top); Lynn Abercrombie/National Geographic: cover
Ivy Images: Nik Wheeler: p. 8
Photographers Direct: Christine Osborne Pictures: p. 17 (bottom)
Photolibrary: Robert Harding Travel: p.5 (bottom)
Rex Features: Sabah Arar: p. 9, p. 23 (top); Denis Cameron: p. 22
Reuters: Faleh Kheiber: p. 26 (bottom); Mohanned Faisal: p. 28 (bottom); Stinger: p. 25 (top)

Map
Jim Chernishenko

Illustrations
Dianne Eastman: icon
David Wysotski, Allure Illustrations: back cover

Back cover: Carp swim in almost every stream, river, and lake in Iraq, and they are raised on fish farms. Most carp caught in Iraq are eaten locally.

Library and Archives Canada Cataloguing in Publication

Fast, April, 1968-
  Iraq : the land / April Fast. -- Rev. ed.

(Lands, peoples, and cultures series)
Includes index.
ISBN 978-0-7787-9279-6 (bound).--ISBN 978-0-7787-9649-7 (pbk.)

    1. Iraq--Description and travel--Juvenile literature.
I. Title. II. Series: Lands, peoples, and cultures series

DS70.65.F38 2010   j956.7   C2009-905132-X

Library of Congress Cataloging-in-Publication Data

Fast, April, 1968-
  Iraq. The land / April Fast. -- Rev. ed.
    p. cm. -- (The lands, peoples, and cultures series)
  Includes index.
  ISBN 978-0-7787-9649-7 (pbk. : alk. paper) -- ISBN 978-0-7787-9279-6 (reinforced library binding : alk. paper)
  1. Iraq--Geography--Juvenile literature. I. Title. II. Series.

DS70.64.F37 2010
956.7--dc22
                                                    2009034653

Crabtree Publishing Company

www.crabtreebooks.com   1-800-387-7650

Printed in China/122009/CT20090915

Published in Canada
Crabtree Publishing
616 Welland Ave.
St. Catharines, ON
L2M 5V6

Published in the United States
Crabtree Publishing
350 Fifth Ave.,
59th Floor
New York, NY 10118

Published in the United Kingdom
Crabtree Publishing
Maritime House
Basin Road North, Hove
BN41 1WR

Published in Australia
Crabtree Publishing
386 Mt. Alexander Rd.
Ascot Vale (Melbourne)
VIC 3032

Contents

 # The cradle of civilization

In the heart of the Middle East, the region bordering the southern and eastern shores of the Mediterranean Sea, lies an ancient land, now called Iraq. Once named Mesopotamia, it was home to the world's first cities and became known as "the cradle of civilization."

A land of riches

Mesopotamia is the Greek word for "land between the rivers." The Tigris and Euphrates rivers, which run through Iraq, have sustained life in this extremely dry region for thousands of years. The rivers are not the country's only valuable resource: Iraq's greatest source of wealth is oil.

Control of the land

Over thousands of years, many peoples and countries have fought over Iraq. Beginning 6,000 years ago, mighty **empires**, including those of the Sumerians, Babylonians, and Assyrians, sought to conquer more land around the Tigris and Euphrates, which were major trade routes. In the 1900s, foreign powers ruled the country.

More recently, tensions between **ethnic** groups within Iraq as well as battles between Iraq and its neighbors have kept the country in a state of war and unrest.

(top) Baghdad is the political, economic, and manufacturing center of Iraq.

Facts at a glance

Official name: Republic of Iraq (Al-Jumhuriya al-'Iraqiya)
Area: 168,754 square miles (437,072 square kilometers)
Population: 28.2 million
Capital city: Baghdad
Official languages: Arabic, Kurdish (in Kurdish regions)
Currency: Iraqi dinar
Official religion: Islam

Crude, or unprocessed, oil is made into gasoline, chemicals for plastic, and other useful products at large factories called oil refineries.

Qurna is a town in Iraq that sits at the point where the Tigris and Euphrates rivers meet. Qurna means "corner" in the Arabic language.

The founding of Iraq

The modern state of Iraq was created in 1921. At first, it was ruled by Great Britain, but it became an independent country in 1932.

British rule

During World War I (1914–1918), the British and their **allies** gained control of Mesopotamia and other lands of the **Ottoman Empire**. The lands were carved into several countries, including Iraq, which was mandated to Great Britain. A mandate is an order for one country to rule on behalf of another country, until it can rule itself.

Merging into one

The people of Iraq came from different ethnic and religious backgrounds, including Arabs in the central and southern regions and Kurds in the north. These groups resented British rule. In addition, they were unhappy that Great Britain named Faisal I, an outsider from a nation now known as Saudi Arabia, as Iraq's king. Many Iraqis **rebelled** against the new leader. In 1958, the royal family was killed in an uprising. A series of weak governments took control of the country, but in 1968, the Ba'th Socialist Party came into power.

Fight for control continues

Iraqis continued to struggle with unrest, both inside and outside the country. Iraq's two main **Muslim** groups, the Sunnis and Shia, struggled to find a balance of power where both groups felt equally significant. Iraq also battled nearby countries. From 1980 to 1988, Iraq fought a bitter war with Iran, its neighbor to the east, over territorial boundaries and threats by Iran to overthrow Iraq's government. In 1990, Iraq invaded neighboring Kuwait for its oil and fought the Persian Gulf War, with Kuwait's allies, including the United States.

Saddam Hussein

Throughout the 1980s and 1990s, a harsh leader named Saddam Hussein ruled Iraq. He tortured and killed those who opposed his rule. On April 9, 2003, armed forces led by the United States and Great Britain overthrew Hussein's government, but this did not bring peace to the country. Establishing a new government created new challenges; violence often broke out among Iraqis, and between Iraqis and the foreign soldiers who had helped overthrow Hussein. The result has been an uncertain future for the people of Iraq.

Faisal I was king of Iraq from 1921 to 1933.

6

Saddam Hussein waves to his supporters in Baghdad. In the first days of his presidency, Hussein had many political rivals and enemies executed.

Iraqi Kurdistan

During World War I, the British promised the Kurds, who lived in a northern region known as Kurdistan, an independent state in exchange for their help in fighting the war. This promise was never fulfilled. Instead, in 1923, Kurdistan was divided among several countries, including Iraq, Iran, Turkey, and Syria.

Since then, violent battles have broken out between the government of Iraq and the Kurds, who want an independent country. On March 11, 1974, after many years of negotiations, the Iraqi government formed the Kurdish Autonomous Region, also known as Iraqi Kurdistan, in the north and northeast. Kurds were given more control of their land and were appointed to key posts in the national government. Kurdish was made the official language of their region. Some Kurds do not think this is enough and are determined to gain the independent country they were promised.

In 1991, the Iraqi government battled Kurds in the north who were seeking greater independence. Thousands of Kurds were killed and many more fled to neighboring Turkey. The United Nations (UN) established a no-fly zone over the area, prohibiting planes from flying overhead and dropping bombs on the people.

A tale of two rivers

Iraq is bordered by Iran in the east, Jordan and Syria in the west, Turkey in the north, and Kuwait and Saudi Arabia in the south. Except for 12 miles (19 kilometers) of coastline along the Persian Gulf in the south, the country is completely landlocked, or surrounded by land.

Tigris and Euphrates

In a country that is mostly desert, the Tigris and Euphrates rivers have been Iraq's main source of water for thousands of years. In ancient times, the rivers were connected by **canals** and **channels**, which **irrigated** the land between them.

Both rivers begin in the snowy mountains of Turkey and flow southeast. The Tigris flows directly into Iraq, while the Euphrates first winds through Syria.

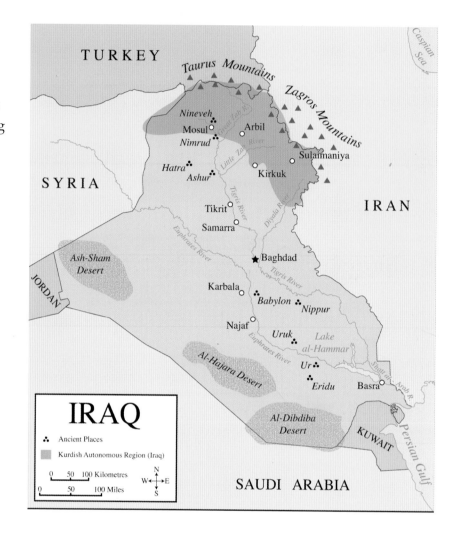

The Euphrates is the longer river, running 1,460 miles (2,350 kilometers), while the Tigris runs 1,150 miles (1,851 kilometers). Even though the Tigris is the shorter and narrower river, it carries more water than the Euphrates because it is fed by other waterways. Mountain rivers, such as the Great Zab, Little Zab, and Diyala, feed the Tigris as it flows along the Zagros Mountains in the northeast.

(left) The Tigris and Euphrates rivers meet to form the Shatt al-Arab River, which runs 100 miles (160 kilometers) before emptying into the Persian Gulf.

Boats traveling along Iraq's rivers carry passengers and cargo.

Floods

The Tigris and Euphrates have sustained life for thousands of years, providing much-needed water for drinking and farming. They have also caused a lot of destruction. Melting snows from the mountains, combined with spring rains, cause the rivers to flood, especially in March, April, and May. During the spring thaw, the Tigris can rise at a rate of one foot (30 centimeters) per hour and cause floods up to 33 feet (10 meters) deep. The Iraqi government has built a series of dams on the Tigris and Euphrates to control flooding and contain water for irrigation. The dams are also used to create **hydroelectric power**.

A fight for water

Iraq is not the only country in the dry Middle East that relies on the waters of the Tigris and Euphrates. People in Turkey and Syria also depend on them for survival. Both Turkey and Syria have built dams on the rivers, which means that less water flows into Iraq. Fights over water are common in the region.

 # From mountains to plains

In northern Iraq, the melting snow from towering mountains gives life to rushing rivers. This terrain gives way to the rolling hills, deserts, and plains of the south.

High in the mountains

Snow-topped mountains in northern Iraq, ranging in height from 8,000 to 11,000 feet (2,440 to 3,350 meters), make up about 20 percent of the country. Iraq's two main mountain chains are the Taurus, on the border with Turkey, and the Zagros, on the border with Iran. Basins created by ancient rivers

separate the two mountain chains. The rivers have also made deep cuts, called gorges, into the rocky terrain.

The mountains are the only parts of Iraq that still have forests. Over the years, many of Iraq's woodlands have been cut down and used for fuel. The Ba'th government also destroyed forests where Kurds once hid from **persecution**.

(top) People live in valleys separating mountain chains. They grow crops, such as wheat and barley, on land made fertile by melting snow and heavy rainfall.

10

Plains

The lower Tigris and Euphrates rivers flow through an area of plains that covers almost one-third of Iraq. The plains were built up over time by swiftly flowing rivers that flooded the land and deposited mud and **sediment**. As a result of continued flooding in some areas, many swampy lakes and marshes, such as Lake as-Saniya and Lake al-Hammar, formed in the region. Reeds, geraniums, rice, and grassy plants called sedges grow in the marshlands. For more than 6,000 years, the marshes have been home to a **semi-nomadic** people known as the Ma'dan.

Disappearing marshlands

More than 90 percent of Iraq's marshlands have disappeared. Rivers and streams in this area were dammed for irrigation, blocking floodwaters from reaching the marshes. The low water levels led to evaporation, leaving salts from the soil to form a crust on the surface. This salty crust destroyed much of the plant and animal life in the marshes. Beginning in 1992, the marshlands were further damaged by the government, which drained the waters to destroy the homes of people who opposed the government.

With the destruction of the marshlands, the people who lived there, the Ma'dan, were no longer able to follow their traditional lifestyle. They could not fish for food, and fewer reeds were available for building homes. As many as 100,000 Ma'dan were forced to leave the marshes to make homes elsewhere. Today, aid organizations are trying to reflood the marshes so that the Ma'dan can return to their lands.

Before the swamplands were drained, the Ma'dan lived on artificial islands built of reeds, palm branches, and mud. They also used tightly bound reeds to make flat-bottomed boats, then covered the reeds in a sticky tar called bitumen, to keep the boats waterproof.

Deserts

Dry, hot deserts cover the western and southwestern parts of Iraq. In western Iraq, the Ash-Sham desert sits more than 1,600 feet (490 meters) above sea level. In the southwest, the Al-Hajara desert is marked with deep ridges. The sandy Al-Dibdiba, in the southeast, is covered with small shrubs. In spring, plants such as spear grass, rock rose, and salt bushes grow for a short time, providing food for sheep, goats, and camels.

Oases

Throughout Iraq's deserts are wadis and oases. Wadis are stream beds that are dry for most of the year but, during the rainy winter, fill with water when sudden floods rage through the land. Oases are fertile areas in a desert. They occur when water trapped in rock deep underground is released on the surface through a crack in the earth or a deep well. In the middle of the desert, this water supports human life and feeds vegetation such as date palms, vegetables, wheat, and barley.

(top) Travelers trek through the desert toward the ancient city of Nippur. The seeds and roots of many desert plants lie dormant for years, ready to sprout and flower after it rains.

A hot, dusty land

Iraq is mostly hot and dry, yet depending on the region and season, it can be rainy, cool, or even snowy. The mountains, plains, and deserts each have their own temperature and rainfall patterns.

Plains and deserts

Iraq has two main seasons: summer and winter. The summer, which lasts from May to October, is very hot during the day and cooler at night. The average July temperature in Baghdad, on the plains of central Iraq, is 95° Fahrenheit (35° Celsius), but temperatures have reached as high as 123° Fahrenheit (51° Celsius). Rain does not fall from June through September. Summer temperatures in the desert soar to 104° Fahrenheit (40° Celsius) during the day, and drop to 68° Fahrenheit (20° Celsius) at night.

Winter is the rainier season, with about four to seven inches (10 to 18 centimeters) of rain, mostly from November to April. Winter weather on the plains is quite mild. The average January temperature in Baghdad is 50° Fahrenheit (10° Celsius). Temperatures in the desert reach 61° Fahrenheit (16° Celsius) during the day, and fall to 48° Fahrenheit (9° Celsius) at night.

Children cool off in the Euphrates River on a hot afternoon.

In the mountains

The mountains in the north have shorter summers and longer winters than the plains and deserts. Summers are usually dry, with temperatures in the city of Mosul averaging 77° Fahrenheit (25° Celsius). The average January temperature in Mosul is 44° Fahrenheit (7° Celsius). Winter temperatures drop even lower when cold winds blow from the northeast.

The mountains and **foothills** receive up to 22 inches (56 centimeters) of **precipitation** each year, mostly during the winter. Heavy winter snowfalls are common in higher areas. When the snow melts in spring, the water flowing down the mountains causes severe flooding in central and southern Iraq.

Young men play in a snow-covered public garden in the Kurdish city of Sulaimaniya.

A boy carefully explores a flooded area after heavy rain in the southern city of Nasiriya.

14

During a drought, important food crops, such as wheat, cannot grow.

Droughts

A drought is a period of unusually dry weather in which little or no rain falls. Rivers and lakes throughout the country dry up, as do the irrigation channels that they supply. Crops fail and people do not have enough food to eat. All that remains is dust, which sweeps through the air as heavy winds blow. The severe drought of 1999 was one of the worst droughts Iraq has experienced, resulting in a shortage of clean drinking water and failed crops. The government relied on goods bought from other countries to help feed the people.

Winds

The *shamal* is a wind that blows through Iraq during the summer for days on end. The temperatures it creates are blistering hot, even though the wind comes from the north. The *shamal* carries such dry air that clouds cannot form. This allows the sun's heat to beat down on the land.

The *sharqi* is a wind from the south and southeast that blows in early summer and early winter. It is stronger than the *shamal*, but does not blow as constantly. The gusts of *sharqi* can reach 50 miles (80 kilometers) an hour and create severe sand and dust storms. They can destroy houses and crops and uproot trees.

Sand and dust storms

Sand and dust storms rage for 20 to 50 days each year, mostly in the summer. Sandstorms occur when strong winds blow sand and **silt** from river basins along the ground. As the winds pick up speed, the grains of sand begin bouncing up and down, colliding with one another, and forming "clouds" close to the ground. Sandstorms can reach heights of 50 feet (15 meters). Dust storms form when dust and tiny pieces of silt are blown high into the air, to an average height of 3,000 to 6,000 feet (900 to 1,800 meters).

Both types of storms cause large problems in Iraq. Sand and dust particles whipping through the air cover skin and wear away at clothing. They get into buildings, food, and drinking water, and work their way into machinery and electronics, damaging wires and equipment. People find it difficult to see through sand and dust storms. Some storms are so severe that airports suspend all flights to prevent any accidents.

A haze shrouds downtown Baghdad as a dust storm blows across the city.

The people of Iraq

The two main ethnic groups that live in Iraq are the Arabs and the Kurds. The Arab people originated in the Arabian Peninsula, in the southwestern corner of Asia. They invaded Mesopotamia in 636 A.D., bringing with them their language, Arabic, and their religion, Islam. Today, Arabs make up 75 to 80 percent of Iraq's population.

Muslims

Iraq's population is 97 percent Muslim. Muslims, or followers of Islam, believe in one God, whose name in Arabic is Allah. Muslims follow the teachings of Allah's **prophets**, the last of whom was Muhammad. There are two main branches of Islam in Iraq: Sunni and Shi'i. Sixty to sixty-five percent of Iraqis are Shia Muslims. They live in the central and southern parts of the country. Sunni Muslims, who make up 32 to 37 percent of the population, live in the central and northern areas. Even though there are fewer Sunnis in the land, they have held power for most of the time since the creation of Iraq.

Devout Muslims pray five times a day to show obedience to Allah and to seek forgiveness and guidance.

Local men spend their time at a café in Duhok, Iraq.

Kurds

More than five million Kurds live in Iraq, making up 15 to 20 percent of the population. Most of them live in the northern and northeastern parts of the country in the Kurdish Autonomous Region. The Kurds are traditionally a semi-nomadic people who raise sheep and goats. Most Kurds are Sunni Muslims. They speak Kurdish, a western Iranian language.

Other peoples

Many other peoples live in Iraq. Turkmen live in the north, near the city of Kirkuk. Most Turkmen are Sunni Muslims. Their **ancestors** were invaders from central Asia, who came to the area in the 1400s. Assyrians live in the northwest. Their ancestors established an empire in Mesopotamia from 1200 B.C. to 612 B.C. Most Assyrians follow a branch of **Christianity** known as the Christian Nestorian Church, while the Chaldean branch of Assyrians belongs to the Roman Catholic Church.

A small population of Armenians live in Baghdad. The first Armenians came in ancient times as traders from Turkey. Armenians also immigrated from Turkey in the 1600s and from Armenia in the 1800s, either to flee religious persecution or because new rulers forced them to leave. Persians, who are mostly Shia Muslims, live around holy cities such as Najaf, Karbala, and Samarra. They came from Persia, which is present-day Iran, to live near the sites where important Shia leaders are buried. The Mandaeans form a small community in southern Iraq and Baghdad and follow a pre-Christian religion called Mandaeanism.

The traditional Kurdish female clothing consists of long dresses of brightly colored fabric and coats embroidered with silver or gold threads.

Ancient cities

Ancient civilizations thrived on the banks of Mesopotamia's rivers, where water was plentiful. The Sumerians, who invented the wheel, **astronomy**, mathematics, and more, built the first cities around 3500 B.C., along the banks of the Tigris and Euphrates. These cities became what are known as city-states, self-governing regions with towns, palm groves, and grain fields. Each of the first city-states had its own ruler and worshiped its own god. Eventually, the city-states were united under one king. Today, archaeologists are uncovering Iraq's ancient cities and working to preserve them for future generations.

Hatra was built in the 100s B.C. and became a major trading center of the Parthian Empire. The Parthians were a people who ruled Mesopotamia from 130 B.C. to 226 A.D.

Eridu

According to legend, Eridu was one of five cities that existed before a great flood swept over the area. The city's god, Enki, the god of water, is believed to have protected the people of Eridu, and the city survived.

In the 1940s, archaeologists began excavating a 19-level tell, or mound that revealed how civilization in Eridu changed over time. Among their findings were 17 mud-brick temples built on top of one another, each more elaborate than the last. Archaeologists also discovered axes, clay figurines, and clay nails. Nearby, a cemetery of 1,000 graves dating back to the 3000s B.C. was found.

Tell-ing the past

Many ancient communities were abandoned or destroyed by invaders, who left mounds of rubble in their wake. Later generations often built new cities right on top of the old ones. This constant building and rebuilding on the same sites created humps on the land called "tells." The tells are made up of several levels, or layers, of ruins. Archaeologists have uncovered many ancient cities under tells, including Ur, whose modern name is Tell el-Muqaiyir, and Nineveh, whose modern name is Tell Kuyunjik. Using special tools and tests, they are able to determine the age of the **artifacts** they uncover and find out how people lived long ago.

In 1895, archaeologists saw tall mounds where the city of Nippur once stood. The tallest mound covered this ancient ziggurat, or temple, dedicated to the god Enlil.

Nippur

The Sumerian city of Nippur was settled around 5000 B.C., south of present-day Baghdad. It became a religious center, with temples devoted to Sumerian gods, especially the supreme god, Enlil. **Pilgrims** flocked there to pray and leave gifts at the temples. Government buildings were built, canals were dug, and walls were constructed to protect Nippur against invaders.

Nippur was abandoned around 800 A.D., but was later discovered beneath a tell 60 feet (18 meters) high and almost one mile (1.6 kilometers) wide. Archaeologists have uncovered the remains of homes, a palace, and temples, as well as stone tablets, bronze statues, jewelry, and pottery.

Ur

Ur became a leading Sumerian city by 2500 B.C. but it started as a simple village on the banks of the Euphrates, in the south. Winding streets lined with homes, stores, and markets were protected from invaders by walls that surrounded the city. Temples, **ziggurats**, storerooms, and a "house of tablets," where laws and records were inscribed on tablets, stood at the city's center.

One of the most important archaeological discoveries made in Ur was an ancient cemetery containing 1,800 graves. Kings, as well as their wives, court officials, and servants, who promised to remain loyal to their rulers in the next life, were buried in 17 of the graves. These graves, known as the Royal Tombs, also contained gifts to the gods, such as gold, silver, jewelry, musical instruments, and collections of artwork.

The most important ziggurat in Ur was dedicated to Nanna, the moon god.

Calah

The ancient city of Calah, known today as Nimrud, was the capital of the Assyrian empire. Tens of thousands of people lived in this northern city amid magnificent temples and palaces.

In 1989, gold and jewelry belonging to four Assyrian queens were found in tombs in Calah. They were placed in the National Museum, in Baghdad, and then moved to an underground safe in the city's Central Bank before the Persian Gulf War, fought with neighboring Kuwait in 1990, broke out. The treasures were rediscovered in 2003 in a vault, undamaged by a flood, **looters**, and **missile** attacks.

Nineveh

Nineveh began as a village around 6000 B.C., near present-day Mosul. Around 700 B.C., the Assyrian king Sennacherib chose it as his capital. He built a huge palace at the center of the city and decorated it with stone **reliefs** showing military victories. Sennacherib's grandson Ashurbanipal built a new palace in Nineveh during his rule, from 668 B.C. to 627 B.C. He also founded a library with more than 20,000 clay tablets or parts of tablets, whose **cuneiform** writings give a glimpse into the law, trade, science, and religion of the time. Ashurbanipal's library was one of the largest and best organized of its time.

The "hanging gardens" of Babylon, shown in this painting, were a gift from Nebuchadnezzar II to his wife, Amytis, who missed her lush, mountainous homeland of Media, in northern Iran.

Babylon

For many years, the city of Babylon was known only in folklore. Tales of "the lost city" prompted archaeologists to search for Babylon for many years. Finally, in the late 1800s Babylon was discovered in the center of present-day Iraq, buried in mud from floods.

Settled on the banks of the Euphrates River in 2200 B.C., Babylon grew into a center of trade and religion. It became the capital of King Nebuchadnezzar II's vast empire in 608 B.C. At the center of the city stood the temple Esagila, dedicated to the Babylonian god Marduk, and the Etemenaki ziggurat, also known as the Tower of Babel. A 700-room palace was protected by the Ishtar Gate, named for the Babylonian goddess of **fertility**, love, and war. Planted on the ledges of a ziggurat just outside the palace was a "hanging garden" made up of thousands of trees, shrubs, and flowers from across the Babylonian empire.

Each of Nineveh's 15 gates was named after an Assyrian god.

Visitors explore the ruins of the ancient Sumerian city of Uruk, built in 4000 B.C. Archaeologists have uncovered walls that once surrounded the city. They have also unearthed 5,000 clay tablets and the ziggurat of Inanna, the goddess of love.

Iraq's disappearing antiquities

Iraq's ancient artifacts and archaeological sites are in danger of being lost or damaged. During times of war, archaeological sites and museums have been **vandalized** and looted, and the treasures stolen from them have been sold to art collectors around the world. Even in times of peace, ancient artifacts have been taken to other countries for display in museums and for private sale.

Lack of funds for the maintenance of Iraq's ancient towns, cities, and riches has also led to their deterioration. Archaeological sites are threatened as new areas of land are cleared for farming and for large construction projects, such as the building of dams. Archaeological agencies around the world are urging people to protect Iraq's ancient sites, monuments, and artifacts and to return Iraq's treasures to Iraq.

Panels that decorated the original Ishtar Gate in Babylon now stand in the Pergamon Museum in Berlin, Germany.

 # Cities north and south

Some of Iraq's modern cities were once home to ancient civilizations, while others were established more recently. These centers of politics, business, and religion have been damaged over time by floods, sand and dust storms, and years of war.

Baghdad

Baghdad, on the western bank of the Tigris River, became the capital of a great Muslim empire in 762 A.D. It was known as "the Round City" because a deep ditch and three circular walls surrounded it. A royal palace and **mosque** stood at the center of the city. Four main roads led out of the city to surrounding areas.

Baghdad was built along trade routes and became a center for business and commerce. Merchants in Baghdad sold pottery from China, spices and dyes from India, gems from Turkestan, ivory and gold dust from East Africa, and pearls and weapons from Arabia. Between 800 and 1100 A.D., Baghdad was known as a

center of learning and culture. Scientists made advances in medicine and astronomy, and **scholars** translated the works of Greek **philosophers** into Arabic. In 1258, the great city was completely destroyed by invaders. Baghdad was rebuilt, but it never regained its past glory.

In 1920, Baghdad became the capital of modern Iraq. Throughout the 1900s, schools, hospitals, banks, and museums were built, mounds of earth and stone, called *bunds*, were constructed to protect against floods, new sewers and waterlines were laid, and superhighways were constructed. Today, although much of the city has been modernized, ancient mosques, palaces, **shrines**, and large, busy *souks*, or outdoor markets, still stand.

(top) Over time, Baghdad expanded, first beyond its walls, to an area known as al-Karkh, then across to the Tigris' eastern bank, to an area called Rusafa.

Mosul

Located on the western bank of the Tigris, in northwestern Iraq, Mosul was an important commercial center along the trade route between central Asia, Persia, and the Mediterranean Sea. The city's name inspired the name of the cotton fabric "muslin," traditionally woven there. Today, grains, fruit, cotton, and sugar cane are grown near Mosul, while oil production and cement manufacturing are important industries.

Mosul still has a traditional feeling to it, with mosques, churches, and tombs dating back several hundred years. The Great Mosque of Nur al-Din, also called Al-Jami al-Kabir, was built around 1170 A.D. It is famous for its leaning **minaret**, called Al-Hadba, and beautiful brickwork. The *mashhad*, or shrine, that honors the religious leader Yahya ibn al-Qasim was constructed in 1239 A.D. It has a pyramid-shaped roof on an octagonal base.

Clothes for sale are displayed on a street in central Baghdad.

Mosul has many modern buildings and structures, in addition to ancient ones, including the University of Mosul and a bridge across the Tigris that leads to vast new suburbs.

Basra

Since ancient times, Basra has been Iraq's main port, from which people and goods come and go on commercial trading ships and military vessels. The main **export** shipped from there is oil. Basra is located on the Shatt al-Arab River, 75 miles (120 kilometers) from the Persian Gulf. The caliph Omar, a religious and political leader, founded Basra as a military camp in 638 A.D.

Today, Basra is made up of three main areas. Ashar is the old commercial center, and includes a market that sells a mix of modern housewares and traditional crafts. Basra is the old residential area. It is still used for housing and is being restored to its former glory. Margil is the port area and has more modern homes.

Irbil

Irbil, also known as Arbil or Hawler, is in the foothills of northern Iraq, in the Kurdish Autonomous Region. Sitting on a tell called Al-Kala'a which rises 100 feet (30 meters) above ground level, it is one of the oldest and continually populated places in the world. Today, Irbil is home to Christians and Sunni Muslim Kurds and Arabs. It is an agricultural center, surrounded by groves of walnut, almond, apple, and pear trees.

(top) Ships continuously shuttle back and forth on the Shatt al-Arab River, to the port in Basra.

Kirkuk

Under Assyrian rule, the city of Kirkuk was called Arrapha. It has developed into one of Iraq's largest modern cities thanks to its fast-growing oil industry. Long pipelines carry oil from Kirkuk through Syria, Lebanon, and Turkey to the Mediterranean Sea. The oil is loaded onto tankers and shipped to other countries. Many people have moved from the countryside to Kirkuk to work in the oil industry. The city is also a center of cloth manufacturing. Kurds, Turkmen, and Arabs live there in roughly even numbers.

Sulaimaniya

The northern city of Sulaimaniya lies around 3000 feet (900 meters) above sea level, within a chain of lush mountains. It is the thriving trade center of Iraqi Kurdistan and the center of Kurdish cultural life. The university in Sulaimaniya has a department of Kurdish language studies, and many cultural festivals are held in the city every year.

Pilgrims in ancient times believed that the sun reflecting on the glimmering gold domes of shrines, such as this one in Karbala, was the light of the imam beckoning them to come.

Shoppers flock to a market in Kirkuk where vendors sell sheep, cereals, olives, fruits, cotton, and other local products. Kirkuk is built on a mound containing the remains of a settlement dating back to 3000 B.C.

Holy cities

The Shi'i consider certain cities in Iraq holy because Shia *imams*, or religious leaders, were buried there. Najaf and Karbala, two of the holy cities, are located in the center of the country. Ali, the prophet Muhammad's cousin and son-in-law, was buried in a part of Najaf called Kufa, and Ali's son Hussein and his half-brother Abbas were buried in Karbala. Today, the cities' large shrines, with their magnificent gold domes and minarets, attract millions of pilgrims every year, many from Iran and India.

Crops and livestock

Iraq has very fertile ground, but less than 15 percent of the total land area is used for farming. The land is most fertile in the foothills, where rainfall is plentiful, and in the central and southeastern parts of the country, where the waters of the Tigris and Euphrates irrigate the land. Iraq's main crops are barley, wheat, rice, dates, tobacco, and cotton. Dates are the country's second largest export, after oil.

Choice crops

In the fall, Iraqi farmers plant grains, such as wheat and barley, which they harvest in the spring. Barley is an especially good crop for the south because it can grow in the salt that builds up in the soil. Large rice fields have also been planted in marshy areas in the south.

Throughout Iraq, vegetables such as beans, eggplant, okra, cucumbers, and onions, grow. Fruits, such as oranges and lemons, are grown in the central and eastern parts of the country. Apples, pomegranates, grapes, olives, and pears are grown in Kurdistan. These crops are planted in the spring and harvested in the fall.

(top) A farmer prepares to ship his corn supply to markets in Iraq. Iraqi farmers either own small plots of land or lease land from the government.

(left) Fishers use nets to catch fish in the Shatt al-Arab River. Iraq has a small fishing industry consisting mostly of freshwater species.

Date palms produce between five and ten bunches of dates per tree. A single bunch may contain more than a thousand dates and can weigh up to 18 pounds (seven kilograms).

Dates

Date palms grow in central and southern Iraq, where temperatures are hot and the soil is sandy. The trees, which grow to heights of 75 feet (23 meters), produce fruit after their fifth to eighth year. This sweet fruit is eaten fresh or dried or is used in cooking and baking. The date tree is often called the "tree of life" because it has so many uses. For example, its leaves, called palm fronds, are used to weave baskets and rugs, and its wood is used to build houses and fences.

Livestock

Many Kurds and Bedouin, a traditionally nomadic people who live in Iraq's deserts, raise sheep and goats for their meat, milk, wool, and skins. Herders in northern Iraq spend winters with their flocks in villages at the foot of the mountains. When spring comes and the snow melts, they take their sheep and goats to feed in the lush pastures of the higher peaks.

The Bedouin raise camels in the southern deserts of Iraq. These desert animals are used for transportation, and their hides and hair are used to make clothing and tents. Other livestock raised in Iraq include water buffalo, which are herded in the southern marshes, and poultry. Cattle are raised in the plains of northern and western Iraq.

Arabian horses

Some breeders in Iraq raise Arabian horses. These intelligent, fast, graceful animals are occasionally used for light work, such as pulling buggies, but they are mainly ridden in the show ring. Most Arabian horses are reddish brown, but gray, chestnut, and brown are also common colors. White markings on the face and legs are also typical. In the past, Arabian horses were a chief Iraqi export to India.

A young girl herds sheep in the southern city of Nasiriya.

Trade and industry

(above) Gas that cannot be used is burned off through pipes called flares. Flaring is also a way to reduce the pressure of gas in the ground.

Iraq's **economy** depends heavily on its **natural resources**: natural gas, phosphates, sulfur, and especially oil. Oil was first discovered in Iraq in 1927. Since then, it has become Iraq's most important source of wealth and largest export.

Oil

Oil is formed underground over millions of years. When the plates that make up Earth's crust shift, their edges bend downward, forming basins that fill with mud. Over time, the mud hardens into rock. Swamp vegetation buried in the mud breaks down, slowly turning into oil and natural gas. The result is rock that is filled with pockets of oil and gas, called source rock. Iraq's main oil fields are in the southeast, just inland from the Persian Gulf. There are also large oil fields in the northern part of the country, near Mosul and Kirkuk, and smaller fields in the west.

Workers in Baghdad's factories produce tractors, construction materials, electronic equipment, furniture, processed foods and beverages, cloth and clothing, and military hardware.

This pipeline pumps oil from Kirkuk to an oil export company in Ceyhan, Turkey. Pipelines also carry oil to power generators that create electricity for Iraqis.

Drilling for oil

Crude oil is the liquid that is brought from the ground and later processed into oil. Once crude oil is discovered, an oil rig is set up to drill a hole into the ground, creating a well. Natural pressure forces crude oil through the well, to the surface, and into tanks. When the pressure is not strong enough, a pump draws the oil to the surface. Then, the crude oil is transported in long pipelines across the country to factories called oil refineries. There, the oil is purified and processed into products such as gasoline, a liquid that fuels automobiles, and propane, a flammable gas that fuels gas stoves and heats homes.

Oil production today

According to scientists, about 112.5 billion barrels of proven, or confirmed, crude oil is beneath the ground in Iraq. An additional 200 billion barrels is thought to be in the ground. As one of the world's largest producers of oil, Iraq is a member of the Organization of Petroleum Exporting Countries (OPEC). OPEC, which includes oil-producing countries from Africa, Asia, the Middle East, and Latin America, determines how much refined oil each country will produce each year.

A suffering economy

Damage to oil wells and refineries during the Iran-Iraq War caused Iraq to lose its major source of income. After the fighting ended in 1988, new pipelines were constructed, oil production facilities were restored, and oil exports gradually increased.

The improvement in the economy did not last long. After Iraq seized Kuwait during the Persian Gulf War, many Arab and western countries joined together to force Iraq out of Kuwait. They introduced economic sanctions, or restrictions, that limited the amount of oil that countries could buy from Iraq. The sanctions were meant to damage Iraq's economy so that it would not have money to produce weapons. Unfortunately, the sanctions had a serious effect on the Iraqi people. They no longer had enough money to purchase medicine and food.

The worldwide community became concerned about the impact of the sanctions on the everyday life of Iraqis. In 1996, the **United Nations** made a deal with Iraq that allowed the country to sell a limited amount of oil overseas and use the money to buy food and medicine. This was called the Oil-for-Food program. Much of the money never reached Iraqis who were most in need. Instead, it went to high-ranking government officials and Saddam Hussein's close associates. Economic sanctions were finally lifted in 2003, after Hussein's regime was overthrown, but economic problems remain as Iraqis try to rebuild their country.

Wildlife

Iraq's wildlife has adapted to the country's wide range of weather and geographic conditions. Some plants and animals have learned to live in the cold, uneven terrain of the mountains. Others have learned to live with very little water in the deserts.

Plants and trees

Hawthorns, junipers, terebinths, and wild pear trees grow on lower mountain slopes. The upper grasslands support plants such as mugwort, goosefoot, milkwood, and thyme. The most fertile land along the banks of the Tigris and Euphrates is home to willows, poplars, alders, and licorice plants. In drier areas, oasis palm trees and camel-thorn shrubs grow. The date palm tree dominates the landscape throughout the country, except in the most northern areas.

Animals

Iraq is home to cheetahs, antelope, gazelles, foxes, wild boars, and hyenas. Hyenas' strong teeth crush the bones of their **prey**, and their howls sound like laughter. Bears, wolves, and leopards live in mountainous areas. Leopards, which are good climbers, often store the remains of animals they kill high up in trees. Fish such as carp and sturgeon swim in the country's rivers and lakes. Carp is used to make a popular dish called *mazgouf*.

Many animals, including the ostrich and wild boar, face **extinction** in Iraq due to the drainage of the wetlands. Others such as the lion and a type of antelope called the oryx are already extinct.

Veiled chameleons change color depending on the temperature, light, and even their emotions. They become paler in cold weather, darkness, or when afraid, and they become darker in hot weather, bright light, or when angry.

30

Desert animals

Iraq's deserts are full of animal life at night, but during the heat of the day, many animals sleep in caves and burrows. Jackals hunt small animals, such as rodents and young gazelles, at night. They also feed on dead animals that other animals have killed. Hairy, golfball-sized camel spiders run at lightning speed to catch their prey. Deadly scorpions crawl along the desert floor, ready to protect themselves with their curved tails tipped with stingers full of venom, or poison. The venom carried by Iraq's saw-scaled viper snake is among the most poisonous in the world.

Up in the air

Many types of birds of prey fly through Iraq's skies, including buzzards, ravens, owls, falcons, eagles, hawks, and vultures. Vultures eat garbage and carrion, or dead animals, tearing the meat apart with their strong beaks. Other birds in Iraq include ducks, geese, partridges, and sandgrouses. Adult sandgrouses often fly long distances, sometimes as far as 25 miles (40 kilometers), looking for water to drink. After they fill up, they wet their breast feathers to carry water to their chicks. Since the draining of the marshes, many birds that once made the marshlands their home are now endangered, or threatened.

Cheetahs can run 70 miles (113 kilometers) per hour, making them the fastest animals on land. Their long, powerful tails help them keep their balance when changing directions at high speeds. Cheetahs face a high risk of extinction in Iraq.

The wild donkey is just one species that has adapted to life in the desert, relying on the bits of grass, herbs, and bushes it finds for food.

Glossary

ally A country that helps another country, especially during a war

ancestor A person from whom another person or group is descended

artifact An object made and used by an earlier culture

astronomy The science of the stars, planets, and moons

canal A human-made waterway

channel A narrow body of water between two areas of land

Christianity The religion that follows the teachings of God and Jesus Christ

cuneiform A type of writing that uses shapes instead of letters

economy A country's system of organizing and managing its businesses, industries, and money

empire A group of countries or territories under one ruler or government

ethnic Relating to groups with the same nationality, customs, religion, or race

export An item sold to another country

extinction The process in which the last remaining animals in a species die off

fertility The capacity to grow, as with plants, or have children

foothill A hill at the base of a mountain

hydroelectric power Electricity produced by fast-moving water

irrigate To supply water

looter A thief

minaret A tower of a mosque from which a person, called a muezzin, traditionally calls Muslims to prayer

missile A rocket used as a weapon to strike a target and explode

mosque A Muslim house of worship

Muslim A person who follows the religion of Islam

natural resource An object found in nature that is of great value to humans

Ottoman Empire Turkish empire that ruled parts of the Middle East, Europe, and North Africa from the 1300s to the 1900s.

persecution The act of harming someone for religious, racial, or political reasons

philosopher A person who studies truth, right and wrong, and the meaning of life

pilgrim A person who makes a religious journey to a holy place

precipitation Water that falls to the earth as rain, snow, hail, or mist

prey An animal killed by another for food

prophet A person believed to deliver messages from God

rebel To fight against an authority

relief A type of art in which designs are raised off a background

scholar A learned person

sediment Material that settles at the bottom of water

semi-nomadic Living in temporary houses and growing crops for one part of the year, and traveling to hunt and gather food for the other part

shrine A holy place, usually a tomb of a holy person

silt Very small pieces of soil and rock that sink to the bottom of water

United Nations An international organization that maintains peace and security around the world

vandalize To destroy or damage something on purpose

ziggurat A pyramid-like tower with a temple on top

Index